EARTH'S CHANGING
WEATHER
and CLIMATE ™

Storms
of the Past and the Future

Karen Donnelly

The Rosen Publishing Group's
PowerKids Press™
New York

To my family: Colleen, Cathy, and David

Published in 2003 by The Rosen Publishing Group, Inc.
29 East 21st Street, New York, NY 10010

First Edition

Editor: Gillian C. Brown
Book Design: Michael J. Caroleo

Photo Credits: Cover, title page, page borders, pp. 7, 8, 19 © Weatherstock/Warren Faidley; Back cover © Digital Vision; pp. 4, 15 (background) © NOAA; p. 11 © Sergio Dorantes/CORBIS; p. 12 © Artville; p. 15 (inset) © NOAA Photo Library, NOAA Central Library; OAR/ERL/National Severe Storms Laboratory (NSSL); p. 16 © CORBIS; p. 20 © Dr. Joseph Golden, NOAA.

Donnelly, Karen J.
Storms of the past and the future / Karen Donnelly.
p.   cm. — (Earth's changing weather and climate)
Includes bibliographical references and index. Summary: This book describes both hurricanes and tornadoes, giving details of storm forecasting and of damages from past storms.
  ISBN 0-8239-6216-4 (lib.)
1. Hurricanes—Juvenile literature 2. Tornadoes—Juvenile literature 3. Storms—Forecasting—Juvenile literature [1. Hurricanes 2. Tornadoes 3. Storms—Forecasting] I. Title II. Series
  QC944.2.D65 2003   2002–000107
  551.55—dc21

Manufactured in the United States of America

Contents

HURRICANE ANDREW
AUG 23, 1992
155 MPH   922 MB

A Bad Storm

On September 8, 1900, people gathered along the beaches of Galveston, Texas, to enjoy the cool breeze and to watch the unusually high waves. In those days before **satellites** and computer-assisted weather **forecasting**, the beachgoers did not know that a deadly hurricane was approaching. When the storm hit, 20-foot (6-m) waves crashed on the beach. Within a few hours, 8,000–12,000 people were killed by the high water, the heavy winds, and the debris.

Today weather forecasters warn that a hurricane is approaching days before it hits land. Most people are able to move out of the hurricane's path. When Hurricane Andrew hit Florida in 1992, 23 people were killed. Many more would have died if the storm had not been forecasted.

This satellite picture of Hurricane Andrew shows the storm over the Bahamas on August 23, 1992, before it slammed into Florida.

The Birth of a Hurricane

Hurricanes are born in the warm, **tropical** air of the southern Atlantic and eastern Pacific Oceans. Most hurricanes develop between late August and early November, after the water has warmed to at least 80°F (27°C). Storms gather heat and moisture from the warm ocean water. Winds near the oceans' surfaces form thunderstorms. Clouds rise high into the sky, sucking the moisture with them. They build as the moisture **condenses** into droplets of rain. The winds **spiral** because of the **Coriolis force**. When the winds reach between 39 and 73 miles per hour (63–117 km/h), a storm is called a tropical depression. A storm becomes a full-grown hurricane when spiraling winds reach 74 miles per hour (119 km/h).

Winds from a hurricane can blow down trees and can damage houses. In Asia hurricanes are also called typhoons.

The Life of a Hurricane

When a hurricane is over warm water, the storm can be active for more than two weeks. Once it moves over land, the storm begins to weaken. Without the moisture from the ocean, the hurricane loses energy. Sometimes, if the hurricane moves back over the water, it can regain strength.

Each year **meteorologists** expect that an average of 10 tropical storms will develop over the Atlantic Ocean, the Caribbean Sea, or the Gulf of Mexico. Of these 10 storms, 6 will probably become hurricanes. Most of these storms will stay over the water. During a three-year period, scientists expect that five hurricanes will strike somewhere along the U.S. Atlantic coastline, anywhere from Texas to Maine.

This picture shows the spiral movement of a hurricane's clouds. The center of the storm, seen here, is called the eye of the storm.

Hurricane Structure

Most hurricanes are more than 300 miles (483 km) wide. They can affect cities and towns far away from the center of the storm. The average hurricane moves forward at 15 to 20 miles per (24–32 km/h).

When a hurricane arrives on land the outer edge of the storm brings rain and winds. For about 4 hours, these winds can rip trees from their roots, can destroy houses, and can tear down power lines. Suddenly the rain and the wind will stop for a few minutes as the calm center of the storm, the eye, passes over. Then the winds will blow again, this time from the opposite direction. Often the second half of the hurricane is more destructive than the first. The weather usually clears 10 hours after the hurricane arrived.

Hurricane Gilbert hit Cancun and southern Mexico in 1988. Enormous waves brought this yacht onto the beach.

Hurricane Damage

Not all hurricane damage is caused by wind. In fact it is the storm surge that often causes the greatest loss of life. A storm surge is a condition of extremely high, powerful waves. The heavy rains also cause flooding. From 6 to 12 inches (15–30 cm) of rain can fall on a location during a typical hurricane. Floodwater levels often continue to rise, even after the hurricane has passed and the weather has cleared.

More than ever before, people are building homes and vacation resorts on the nation's seacoasts. Future hurricanes will probably cause more property damage. Hurricane Andrew caused the most expensive weather-related loss in American history. It caused more than $26 billion in damage, but it was the only hurricane to hit land that year.

Hurricanes create intense ocean conditions, which can create high waves that damage houses close to the shore.

Forecasting Hurricanes

Meteorologists at the National Hurricane Center (NHC) use satellites to forecast hurricanes as they develop. From satellite photographs, meteorologists can tell when storm clouds over the ocean begin to spin. **Doppler radar** is used to track the path of a storm. Scientists also send a radiosonde, a small package of scientific instruments attached to a weather balloon, up into the atmosphere. The radiosonde sends information on **air pressure**, **temperature**, and **humidity** to the meteorologists' computers.

Even with the best information available, it is still difficult to know what a hurricane will do. Climate conditions can change quickly. Meteorologists try to warn anyone who would be in the path of a dangerous storm to get to safety.

This picture shows a doppler radar station. Doppler radar can only "see" 200 miles (322 km) from shore.

The Future of Hurricanes

Some scientists think that for the next 20 or 30 years, warmer temperatures on the surface of the ocean may cause more hurricanes. Meteorologists from the Hurricane Research Division of the National Oceanic and Atmospheric Administration (NOAA) believe that the warmer ocean temperatures are caused by a natural warming cycle. They believe we are at the beginning of this cycle, which lasts from 25 to 40 years. Most scientists believe that it is unlikely that **global warming**, an increase in the average temperatures of Earth, causes more hurricanes. Some **evidence** exists that cooler temperatures may cause an increased number of hurricanes.

The year 1998 was a La Niña year, with cooler ocean temperatures. Ten hurricanes developed in the Atlantic Ocean that year.

Tornadoes

Tornadoes are born from severe thunderstorms. A column of twisting air called a **vortex** rises from the ground to the base of the storm clouds. Most tornadoes last less than 10 minutes. Tornadoes can be seen as twisting funnel clouds that get their color, usually gray, from the dust and the **debris** they suck up from the ground.

Tornadoes move very quickly, about 35 miles per hour (56 km/h). They are much harder to predict than hurricanes. This makes it difficult for people to get out of the way. In the United States, tornadoes happen most often in parts of Texas, Oklahoma, Kansas, Missouri, Nebraska, Arkansas, Iowa, Florida, and Mississippi. Together these states are called Tornado Alley.

The strongest tornadoes are estimated to have wind speeds as high as 261 to 318 miles per hour (420–512 km/h).

Forecasting Tornadoes

Most tornadoes appear on radar only a few minutes to a half hour before they strike. Scientists are still not sure why some thunderstorms cause tornadoes and others do not. Meteorologists at the National Weather Service (NWS) warn of severe thunderstorms that are likely to become tornadoes. The NWS also relies on people known as storm spotters. Storm spotters are trained to report important weather information. They contact the NWS immediately to report a tornado sighting.

The wind speeds where a tornado touches the ground are still largely unknown because getting close to a tornado is very dangerous. Meteorologists estimate the wind speeds of tornadoes based on the kind of damage they do.

A tornado over a lake or an ocean is called a waterspout. This waterspout was photographed near the Florida Keys.

Tornadoes of the Future

The number of recorded tornadoes in the United States has increased dramatically since 1950, when 201 tornadoes were recorded. In 1999, there were 1,342 tornadoes reported. More people report tornadoes now than in the past, which explains the higher numbers.

Climate may affect the number of severe thunderstorms that produce tornadoes. Scientists still do not know how. They are studying whether warmer ocean temperatures cause more tornadoes. Much of the evidence today shows that this is not true. In 1997, when **El Niño** caused warm ocean temperatures, there were 1,148 tornadoes in the United States. In 1998, when **La Niña** caused cooler ocean temperatures, 1,424 tornadoes occurred.

Glossary

air pressure (EHR PREH-shur) The weight of the air. In the atmosphere it is caused by the weight of the air high above Earth pushing on the air closer to Earth.

condenses (kun-DEN-siz) Cools and becomes a liquid.

Coriolis force (kor-ee-OH-lus FORS) The effect Earth's rotation has on things on Earth's surface, such as wind currents and airplanes.

debris (duh-BREE) Trash or scattered remains of something.

doppler radar (DAH-plur RAY-dar) A tool that uses sound waves to track storms.

El Niño (EHL NEEN-yo) A warming of ocean water in the tropical eastern Pacific Ocean. When El Niño becomes strong, it can affect weather worldwide.

evidence (EH-vih-dints) Facts that prove something.

forecasting (FOR-kast-ing) Figuring out when something will happen.

global warming (GLOH-buhl WARM-ing) A gradual increase in the temperature of Earth.

humidity (hyoo-MIH-dih-tee) The amount of moisture in the air.

La Niña (LAH NEEN-yah) A cooling of the ocean water in the central eastern Pacific Ocean. La Niña can affect weather around the world.

meteorologists (mee-tee-er-AH-luh-jists) People who study the weather.

satellites (SA-til-eyets) Spacecrafts that orbit Earth.

spiral (SPEYE-rul) A curve that keeps winding, like the curve of a bedspring.

temperature (TEM-pruh-cher) The degree of hot or cold.

tropical (TRAH-puh-kul) Having to do with the warm parts of Earth that are near the equator.

vortex (VOR-teks) The part of the tornado cloud that points to the ground.

Index

Web Sites

To learn more about storms, check out these Web sites:

www.fema.gov/kids/hurr.htm

www.noaa.gov

www.spc.noaa.gov

24